Hippos

Hippos

by Christina Wilsdon

Reader's Digest

Published by The Reader's Digest Association, Inc.

London • New York • Sydney • Montreal

CONTENTS

Chapter 1

A hippo story

Two big round nostrils poke out of the muddy water of an African lake. Water sprays as a loud snort bursts from them. These nostrils belong to a river hippopotamus that has come up to take a breath.

Suddenly a smaller pair of nostrils pops up nearby. Quickly, they open and suck in air. These nostrils belong to a baby hippo that has just been born. And this is his very first breath.

The hippo calf is only a few minutes old, but he can already walk and swim. He follows his mother to shore on wobbly legs. She turns her enormous head to check on him. No wild animals would dare to attack her, but a hungry crocodile, hyena or lion might try to catch her calf. If one of these predators comes near, Mother Hippo will stand like a wall between it and her baby – or charge at the predator and trample it.

Now Mother Hippo stops so Baby Hippo can drink some milk. As he nurses, his nostrils shut and he holds his breath. The calf does not even think about doing this – it just happens automatically. This kind of automatic action is called a reflex. Hippo calves have this reflex because they often nurse underwater, where they must hold their breath for up to 2 minutes.

Baby Hippo rapidly grows bigger and stronger. He gains as much as 5kg a day!

When he is almost three weeks old, Mother Hippo brings him to the herd. For the first time, he meets other hippo calves and cows. There are about 30 hippos altogether, lolling in the mud and snoozing in the water.

Now Mother Hippo can leave his side for part of the day because he is old enough to join a 'play group' of other calves while she takes a break to eat or nap. This group is called a crèche (pronounced KRESH). The crèche is carefully watched over by a few cows from the herd. These baby-sitter cows are called 'aunts'.

Baby Hippo quickly learns that other calves make great playmates. He tussles with the male calves, opening his mouth wide and biting at them. He plays hide-and-seek with the female calves. All the calves shove and push against each other like puppies, and they splash and roll in the water.

As the calves play, the aunts stand guard, alert for lions and crocodiles. They also carefully watch any bull hippos that come close to the crèche. If the bulls behave too roughly, the cows chase them away.

DID YOU KNOW?

- A female hippo is called a cow.
- A male hippo is called a bull.
- A baby hippo is called a calf.
- A calf weighs 27kg to 45kg when it is born. It is about a metre long and 0.5m high.

By the time Baby Hippo is six months old, he weighs more than 220kg! But he can still climb onto Mother Hippo's back as she rests in the water. Sometimes he dozes on top of her. Other times he uses her as a diving platform, clambering up one side and flopping back into the water on the other.

Mother Hippo nuzzles and nibbles Baby Hippo as she grooms him. She also teaches him proper hippo behaviour. If he misbehaves, she bumps him with her head, nips him, or even knocks him down.

Baby Hippo is now grazing on grass as well as drinking his mother's milk. Soon he will be weaned, which means he will no longer nurse from his mother. When he is eight months old, he will eat only grass and plants.

When he is a year old, he will be able to live on his own – though he will not reach his full size until he is four. Some young males leave the herd to claim their own patch of river. The females stay and will have their first calves when they are about seven years old.

For now Baby Hippo will follow his mother and may stay until he is four years old and as big as she is. Some cows have as many as four youngsters lined up behind them in age order, from youngest to oldest.

DID YOU KNOW?

The word hippo means 'horse' in Greek. The word hippopotamus is made up of two Greek words which put together mean 'river horse'.

The body
of a hippo

A hippo sleeping in water automatically rises to the surface every few minutes for a breath of fresh air, then slowly sinks again.

DID YOU KNOW?

A hippo usually stays underwater for up to 5 minutes. Some people say a hippo can hold its breath for up to 30 minutes!

Like a tank

The hippopotamus is the world's third largest land animal. It can measure up to 4.5m long, about the length of a minivan. Females weigh up to 2,300kg, and some very big males can weigh 3,600kg. The only other land animals that are bigger are the elephant and the white rhinoceros. All three of these giant animals live in Africa.

Four short, thick legs hold up a hippo's barrel-shaped body. Each foot has four toes linked by stretchy flaps of skin. When a hippo walks, the toes spread apart and help it to plod across muddy ground. In the water, these flaps help it to swim, just as webbed feet help a duck to paddle.

A hippo may seem slow and sleepy. But don't let its looks fool you! A hippo can trot as fast as a running person on land. It can gallop nearly as fast as a horse for a short distance. And it does not veer around things. Like a tank, it crashes through them — or over them!

A hippo's weight allows it to walk underwater, right on the bottom of lakes and rivers. A hippo can even leap along the bottom in a series of graceful bounds. This motion is called 'punting'.

Look and listen

Big as a hippo is, sometimes the only parts of it that can be seen are its nostrils. A hippo may stay underwater all day, poking only its nostrils out to breathe. As its eyes are on top of its head, the hippo can also peek above water while hiding under it. Its ears stick out of the water, too.

When a hippo sinks underwater, it closes its nostrils and folds its ears back against its head. This keeps water out of its ears but a hippo can still hear underwater because its jaw helps it to pick up sounds made in the water. The sound waves travel through a pad of fat in its lower jaw, then up through the jawbones and into its ears. A hippo can even tell what direction an underwater sound is coming from by comparing what it 'hears' on the left and right sides of its jaw.

Heavy head

A hippo's head weighs around 450kg – about as much as a horse! The head forms about a third of the hippo's length.

A hippo can hear both above the water and underwater at the same time. Above water, it listens with its ears. Underwater, it picks up sounds with its jaws.

A hippo's tusks can grow to be 75cm long! You can only see part of a tusk because most of it is buried in the jaw.

Open wide!

A hippo's head is mostly mouth; when it yawns, its mouth opens about 1.2m wide!

Inside this mouth are as many as 44 teeth. In front, two large teeth called tusks stick out from the top jaw and two from the bottom. In between the tusks are pointed front teeth called incisors. Tusks and incisors grow throughout the hippo's life. Every time the hippo opens and shuts its mouth, the top and bottom tusks and incisors rub against each other. This rubbing files them down and keeps them from getting too long. It also keeps them sharp, which is important because hippos use them as weapons, not for eating.

A hippo gathers food with its lips. It clamps them around tufts of grass, then swings its head to rip off the blades. Its large tongue shovels the food to the back of its mouth, where rows of ridged, blocky teeth grind the food before it is swallowed.

Skin deep

With sharp tusks in its mouth and a thick layer of fat on its body, a hippo seems like an armoured tank. But its skin is really quite tender. A hippo lacks a fur coat to protect its skin. Its only hair consists of some bristles on its ears, snout and tail. A hippo gets sunburnt quite easily!

Keeping moist is the hippo's only protection against the hot African sun. Wallowing in mud also helps. So does staying underwater during the day. A hippo's skin also oozes a pinkish, oily liquid that helps to keep its skin moist. The liquid works as a sunscreen, too. It also seems to kill germs, like the antiseptic cream you might put on a cut.

Chapter 3

A herd of hippos

These peaceful-looking cows
can become very aggressive
if they think their calves are
threatened or in any danger.

Who's who?

Rows of grey boulders poke up out of the water. Birds step carefully across them, looking for insects but take flight when they move. For the boulders are really the round backs of hippopotamuses, snoozing the day away.

A hippo herd ranges in size from five to a hundred. It is made up of cows and their calves, including newborns and older sisters as males more than a year old often leave.

Each herd has its own place on the riverbank. Cows chase away cows from another herd if they get too close. Powerful bulls stake out parts of the riverbank as their own and each defends his territory against other bulls.

Cows and bulls

Sometimes bulls and cows wrestle with each other in the water. They open their mouths wide and clatter their tusks together. But they are not fighting. All this splashing and clacking is part of hippo courtship. A cow and a dominant bull play with each other in this way before mating. The cow gives birth to her calf about eight months later.

Hippo talk

Hippos live in murky water that is thick with mud and muck. It is hard to peer through it, but hippos do not need to use their eyesight to find out where other hippos are. They often use sound instead.

Scientists who study hippos have discovered that it's noisy underneath the surface. Hippos underwater make all kinds of sounds: croaks, clicks, squeaks, squeals, honks and groans.

Above the water, hippos are noisy, too. A hippo may poke its nostrils out of the water and snort, blowing 'raspberries'. Bulls bellow loudly. Often, when a bull bellows, other bulls up and down the river bellow back.

Staking a claim

Finding and keeping a good territory is a bull's full-time job. A young bull must have his own territory before he can mate with cows and become a father. The best territory is on the edge of the riverbank, next to the water. But these areas are usually already taken by other bulls, known as dominant bulls.

To get a territory like this, a bull must fight with a dominant bull. If he wins, he gets the territory and becomes the dominant bull. If he loses, he will be lucky to escape with his life.

DID YOU KNOW?

A bull bellows to let other bulls know that he is guarding his territory – and they had better stay away.

A bull's bellow is so loud that it creates a throb in the air. Scientists say hippos can feel a bull's bellow as well as hear it.

27

Hippos fight fiercely.
Most adult hippo bulls
are striped with scars
from old battle wounds.

Keep out!

DID YOU KNOW?

Hippos use their teeth for both love and war. Bulls show off their tusks to other bulls. Fighting hippos stab with them. Courting hippos clack each other with them.

A dominant bull spends a lot of energy defending his territory. The bull's defence begins with marking his territory. He marks it on land and in the water with his droppings. Just smelling that a bull owns a territory is enough to make some bulls stay away. The bull also bellows to warn off intruders.

If a bull enters his territory anyway, the dominant bull challenges him. First, he yawns widely at the intruder to show off his enormous tusks. The intruder may yawn back at him. Then the dominant bull snorts and bellows until the intruder leaves or stands and fights.

The two bulls in a fight for territory charge at each other. In the water, each bull uses his lower jaw as a bucket, scooping up water and tossing it at his opponent. The bulls open their mouths wide. They slash at each other with their razor-sharp tusks. They lock teeth and shove each other like two goats locking horns. They snap at each other's front legs. A hippo bull can break another bull's leg if he can get a grip on it.

The fight ends when one bull has had enough — or when one bull is killed. The winner keeps the territory. If the loser survives, he leaves.

A hippo's day

Hippos stay close together during the day, but at night, when they leave the mud and water to graze, they go off alone.

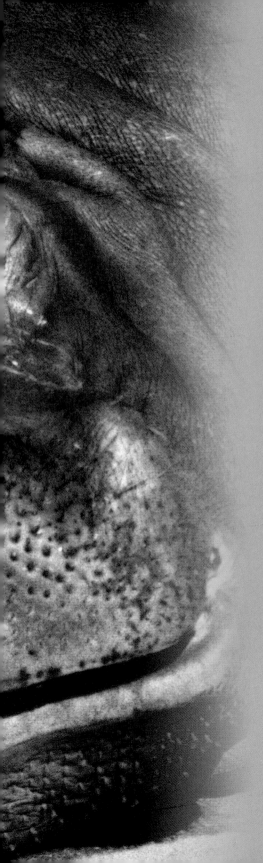

Keeping cool

Hippos spend most of the day lounging in water and lumber ashore occasionally to lie in the sun. They stay in water so long because they lack sweat glands, so they cannot sweat to cool off. If hippos stay out in the hot sun, their skin starts to crack and dry. They can also overheat and get so thirsty that they die.

So a hippo uses the daytime for sleeping and resting in cool water and mud, safe from the sun's burning rays. The water and mud also help to keep biting insects away.

While the hippo naps, it slowly digests the tough grass and leaves it ate the night before. It can take two days for a meal to pass through the hippo's digestive system.

Wake up!

The sun begins to set, and the hippos begin to stir. The calves play. The cows rumble and click to each other below the water. They snort and grumble above it. As the sun sinks in the sky, the hippos rise. They trudge out of the water and up the riverbank. It is time to leave the water and find grass to eat.

Amazing grazing

The hippos follow well-worn paths to the grazing grounds. These paths have been carved out by other hippos over many years. Along the way, the paths branch out into many other paths. Each cow and calf follows a different one. Hippos spend all day with their herd, but at night they graze alone or with just their young.

Rip, rip, rip goes the grass as a hippo swings her head, tearing the blades up with her lips. She will spend about 5 hours eating grass and leaves. She will also eat any fruit she finds lying on the ground. As she grazes, she may wander from 3 to 6 miles.

People who live in areas with hippos know that they must be careful if they go out into the wild at night. They do not want to surprise a grazing hippo. Hippos may look a bit silly, but they are actually one of the most dangerous animals in Africa. A frightened hippo will attack humans as well as other animals.

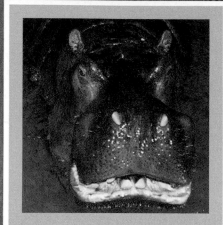

Super-size smile!

A hippo's big lips are rough and strong for grazing on grass. A bull's lips can measure half a metre across.

During a single night's grazing, a hippo will eat 45kg of food!

The river hippopotamus is also known as the common hippopotamus and the **Nile** hippopotamus.

At home in the water

As dawn approaches, the hippos return to the river. They slip into the water to nap the hot day away. Their full stomachs slowly get to work digesting their food. If necessary, the hippos can go for two weeks or more without eating. They are so big and use so little energy all day long that they can make their big meals last a long time.

As they wallow in the water, the hippos also help to make it a better habitat for other animals that live there. They do this simply by digesting their food and producing droppings. Hippo manure works as a fertiliser in the water, helping tiny plants grow. Pond scum, or algae, also grows abundantly, thanks to the hippos' manure. Fish eat the tiny creatures that feed on the algae and plants. Then birds and crocodiles eat the fish.

Every step a hippo takes in the water also helps to feed other water animals. A hippo is so heavy, it can actually walk on the bottom of a river or lake. Its feet stir up mud as it moves. Tiny animals living in the mud are kicked up, too, becoming meals for fish.

Fish also nuzzle along the hippos' sides, nibbling on algae and other titbits clinging to their rough skin. Above the water, egrets and other birds perch on the hippos to pick off and eat ticks and other pests.

DID YOU KNOW?

The river hippopotamus's name is a clue to its main habitat – rivers. Hippos also live in lakes and wetlands. They need deep water sources that do not dry up for part of the year. In times of drought, hippos may be forced to wander long distances to find another habitat.

Chapter 5

Hippos in the world

Little hippo

There are actually two kinds of hippos: the river hippopotamus and the pygmy hippopotamus. The pygmy hippo lives in forests near swamps and rivers. It is much smaller. It is about 1.5m long and stands about 1m tall. It weighs about 225kg – less than a river hippo's head!

Home of the hippos

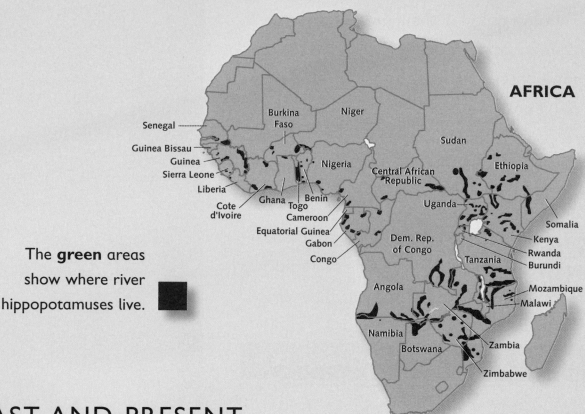

AFRICA

Senegal
Guinea Bissau
Guinea
Sierra Leone
Liberia
Cote d'Ivoire
Ghana
Togo
Benin
Cameroon
Equatorial Guinea
Gabon
Congo
Burkina Faso
Niger
Nigeria
Central African Republic
Sudan
Ethiopia
Uganda
Dem. Rep. of Congo
Angola
Namibia
Botswana
Zambia
Zimbabwe
Tanzania
Somalia
Kenya
Rwanda
Burundi
Mozambique
Malawi

The **green** areas show where river hippopotamuses live.

PAST AND PRESENT

Thousands of years ago, river hippopotamuses lived throughout Africa. They were common in the Nile River of Egypt. The ancient Egyptians feared and respected them.

Hunting by humans, however, caused the disappearance of hippos from northern Africa and parts of western Africa. The spread of deserts and the growth of farms and cities have also made hippo habitats shrink. Today, scientists estimate that there are about 157,000 hippos. They live mainly in East Africa and southern Africa. About 2,000 pygmy hippos survive in Liberia and a few other African countries.

The future of hippos

Hippos used to be hunted only for their meat, which didn't greatly reduce their numbers. But in the 1700s, European explorers also began hunting them for sport. By the early 1800s, thousands of hippos that had lived along the Nile River in Egypt were gone. Today hippos are threatened by those who hunt them illegally for their tusks and meat.

Habitat loss is another threat. Hippos need water and space to graze and roam. The growing human population takes land for farms and towns. Rice paddies are replacing wetlands, and farmers may kill hippos that eat their crops.

FAST FACTS ABOUT RIVER HIPPOPOTAMUSES	
SCIENTIFIC NAME	*Hippopotamus amphibius*
CLASS	Mammals
ORDER	Artiodactyla
SIZE	Males up to 4.5m in length Females up to 4.2m in length
WEIGHT	Males to 3,600kg Females to 2,300kg
HABITAT	Rivers, lakes, wetlands
TOP SPEED	About 30 miles per hour
LIFE SPAN	Up to 40 years in the wild

DID YOU KNOW?

Hippo droppings fertilise plants in the water and help to provide food for fish. The capturing of hippos around one African lake caused its fish populations to drop dramatically. This has created problems for people who live in the area and make their living by fishing.

GLOSSARY OF WILD WORDS

aunt	a hippo cow that baby-sits the calves of other cows		courtship	the behaviour used by male and female hippos to pair up as mates
bull	an adult male hippo		cow	an adult female hippo
calf	a baby hippo		crèche	a group of hippo calves
conservation	the protection and preservation of land, animals, plants and other natural resources		drought	a long period of time without rain
			genus	a large category of related plants or animals consisting of smaller groups (species) of closely related plants or animals

graze	to feed on grass		prey	animals that are hunted by other animals for food
habitat	the natural environment where an animal or plant lives		range	all the places where a species lives
predator	an animal that hunts and eats other animals to survive		species	a group of living things that are the same in many ways
preserves	areas of land or water where wildlife and plants are protected		territory	an area of land or water that an animal considers to be its own and will fight to defend

INDEX

CREDITS

Hippos is an ***All About Animals*** fact book
Written by Christina Wilsdon

Published in 2010 in the United Kingdom by Vivat Direct Limited (t/a Reader's Digest),
157 Edgware Road, London W2 2HR

Editor: Rachel Warren Chadd
Designer: Nicola Liddiard
Art editor: Simon Webb

Printed and bound in Europe by Arvato Iberia

ISBN: 978 0 276 44611 5
Book code: 640-020 UP0000-1
Oracle code: 504500067H.00.24